DIGITAL
NOMAD

BY DAVE BRETT

Digital Nomad
By Dave Brett

Preface - My Story

At the age of 15 I ran away to start a new life in Finland, a crazy decision made after I had experienced a rocky moment in my life. With my childhood savings and a flight ticket in hand, I arranged to stay with Finnish friends I had met the previous summer. After travelling solo around Finland for two months, I quickly discovered how much I enjoyed travelling and meeting other cultures. This one unique experience had changed my life forever and I knew I wanted to continue pursuing my newly discovered passion for exploring the world around me.

Now it's Ten years later and I haven't stopped travelling. I've been to 85+ countries and lived in Finland, Switzerland, the Netherlands, the US, Wales, Singapore and Thailand. I continue to pursue my dream of visiting every country in the world.

All of this has been made possible by being frugal, living a location independent lifestyle, remaining mobile and running an online travel blog to generate an income.

I've put this book, Digital Nomad, together to lay out all the lessons I've learned from living a location independent lifestyle and to offer all the helpful information I've picked up over the years to anyone seeking to do the same.

A Creative Generation is Born

We are lucky that in today's world, those with creative minds can choose to take a different path. With the technology we have now, along with the globally connected world we are living in, those that wish to be rebellious in order to to create a better life, can. It's not a path suited to everyone, but those that wish to choose it have never been in a better situation than now.

If you're reading this book, then you are amongst those few that seek to free themselves. With a better understanding of the landscape, you can choose to follow this path and create a lifestyle that works for you. If you're interested in how this is possible, then this book can also help you visualise the possibilities.

It's not for everyone. It requires a lot of work and self-discipline. The only person you will be failing is yourself and that's the key to success when following this path. You're the only person who can let yourself down and if you take this on board and you're prepared to take the risk, then you are mentally ready to take on this challenge.

If you do fail, and some do, at least you can look back and say "Hey, I tried!". That is a better outcome than never attempting to give it a go and wondering what might've been.

I will be honest, it's tough.

Nothing worth doing in life is easy, but with determination and a willingness to succeed you can make it possible, that's the difference between those that fail and those that flourish. It requires a lot of personal commitment to achieve a self-created lifestyle.

So why not give it a try? You only have yourself to let down. Strive to be the person you want to be, put in the work, and its totally possible.

Failure is never an option, but its always better to learn from mistakes and improve yourself. If you are creative, then use that creativity to get you where you want to be in life. With a little guidance and self discipline you can make it happen.

Travel is a powerful force that only a few get to experience in depth. I'm not talking about going on a week-long all-inclusive holiday to the Maldives. I'm talking about long term travel. Travelling for a long period of time unlocks many different doors that short term travel can't go near. It's a completely different experience and can change you as a person for the better. Don't think you have to be a youngster, fresh out of graduation to make long-term travel work. It's something you can partake in at any stage of your life and career and accessible to all.

The key to long term travel is being frugal with your finances, this is maybe why students are the most common audience for such travel as they tend to be used to stretching a little money a long way. Long term travel tends to require the same values.

Using your skills online can be valuable, as many people seek help on the internet with jobs they can't or won't do themselves. If you are able to use the web to sell your creative skills and create solutions to people's problems, then it's possible to create an income while remaining mobile.

If you can build an audience that wants to use the skills you offer, then you can create an income this way. What's keeping you from staying at home? Why couldn't you run this business on the road using just a laptop and an internet connection?

The Digital Nomad

Becoming a digital nomad means living a minimal lifestyle, finding out what works and what doesn't, and using the money you make to create a freedom lifestyle.

Sure, you can graduate from University, go straight into a full time job and fund a certain lifestyle, but will it give you the freedom you seek?

Being a digital nomad is a new lifestyle choice for independent minds and it could work for you. This is the concept behind this book; to discuss the concept of becoming a digital nomad and determine how to achieve this lifestyle with the skill set you currently possess.

Living out of hand luggage, being able to move freely around the world and looking at life through a different window, this lifestyle will open doors completely different to a location dependent life. It's a freedom lifestyle you can create, alternative for sure, rebellious to some, but it might just be the lifestyle you wanted all along.

If you have a skill that can be utilised or sold to an online audience, then being a location independent Digital Nomad can work for you, like it already does for many that have unlocked this lifestyle for themselves.

Content Page

Content Page

Content Page

What is a Digital Nomad?

The terminology "Digital Nomad" first crossed my path on a blog post I read more than 7 years ago. The moment I started reading, I was captivated by the possibilities of this concept.

Nomads are people that live in remote locations around the world and travel from one point to another. They travel only with what they can carry on their chosen form of transportation, be it a camel, reindeer or Husky sledge. It's a minimal approach to life, yet it offers no limitations or attachments to a set location. Nomads simply have no borders, they adapt to their surroundings and freely move whenever they see fit.

The term Digital Nomad is derived from this, but with the added adoption of technology and the Internet. If you're reading this book, then you most probably have the technology to make this lifestyle possible.

The World Wide Web is Gigantic.

The internet can be a big and scary place. But if you can offer something unique that people want, then you might have a big fish on the end of your hook that you just have to reel in.

What do you value most in life? Might it be a hobby, or something that you're good at? Can you turn this into a business?

For me travelling is my hobby. From the age of 15 I had no idea what my future would hold. Ten years later, I'm still travelling. It's a passion that I was lucky enough to stumble across at a young age and I have never regretted endeavouring into it.

I live to travel, and strive for more. In fact, I never stop thinking about travel. Every day I wake up, eat, sleep and live for travel. For me it was a no brainer to turn this into a business.

You might have a similar interest or passion, too. Could you possibly turn this into a business? Sure, they say it's not a good idea to mix business with pleasure, but when you have so much passion for something, then you should try anything in your power to keep it alive. Many people around the world have hobbies and interests, and use the Internet to seek to improve in that passion.

If you're able to channel your passion towards this crowd, people will look for you and possibly turn into your audience. You can then build a business around gathering your tribe. If you have a skill that an audience also seeks to learn, you can help others to achieve their goals too.

Gone are the days when people went to libraries to seek information. The masses now use the internet for these tasks and, as it continues growing to all corners on the planet, your audience will grow as well.

If you are able to create a desirable product or service, over time that word will spread and your business will start to grow.

Two marathon runners complete in a race. One is the fastest, while the other had the craziest costume, who has the better story? The answer is that they both have great stories that will appeal to different audiences, but they have still competed in the exact same race. It's still possible to stand out in a crowded market and sell the same product if you offer something different, such as your own unique approach.

How I Discovered the Digital Nomad Lifestyle

I read a blog post regarding an individual who had taken on the Digital Nomad lifestyle for six months as an experiment to see if it was possible. He wanted to reset life and start from scratch in order to adapt to becoming a Digital Nomad. It was an interesting experiment that allowed him to travel with just a small bag, passport, a few sets of clothes, a laptop and an affordable round the world (RTW) Ticket.

During these six months he travelled to every continent, while running an online business to fund his new lifestyle. He had already run an online business, with paying clients, from home. He wondered if he could take this business with him to another country without affecting the service he provided. He never told his clients what he was up to in fear that they would no longer work with him. Rather than being glued to a desk in his Manhattan apartment, with high rent costs and expensive coffee shops on every corner, he decided to cancel all his rental agreements and subscriptions, put his business online and hit the road.

He would schedule work times in the week, when he would set out to find coffee shops with good wifi in each location. Sometimes, due to time differences, clients would email him work in the evening and would get the finished job back first thing in the morning, even though he was just working normal office hours at his current location. Clients were impressed by his speed, rather than annoyed. Working in different time zones had its own advantages.

By eating only street food, hitch-hiking and staying on locals couches, he kept his costs low. He travelled with only what he could fit in his small carry-on bag and managed it while travelling around the world. Each week he was putting money into a savings account rather than living from paycheck to paycheck.

After six months were over, he didn't want to return home. His clients, for that matter, hadn't noticed any hiccups at all and were surprised to hear what he had been up to. They noticed an increased level of service with the new deadline system he had put in place rather than the neglect they would have expected had he told them in the first place.

At the start, it took risks and sacrifices to enter a whole new ball park with his business. He could have lost his clients, and he had many hoops to jump through, but over time he adapted his new system, pulled it off, and came out better for the experience.

From paying high rent in NYC, to staying in affordable beach huts around South East Asia, he was spending less, earning the same, and was happier as an outcome.

What started out as an experiment, opened up many people's eyes to what was possible when running online business platforms. With a skill set that can build an audience or gather clients, this lifestyle is a possibility. Your clients won't care where you get the work done, as long as it gets done.

You don't have to change your life to this extent, but it's a great foundation to learn from, and to open up the possibilities to build your own freedom lifestyle.

The Nomad Concept

You could move city to city every 6 months and still gain a similar experience. For a lot of people this is the case - 6 months in Dubai, 6 months in Bangkok, 6 months in Barcelona, 6 months in Singapore, 6 months in Berlin, 6 months in Bali - you get the picture. You also don't have move constantly, you can choose to stay a little longer or embark on a constantly moving adventure to explore the world.

Many cities around the world are now leaning towards adapting to this new mobile working environment and supporting this lifestyle by offering business tech hubs called Co-Working spaces, where you can go to run your business for a short amount of time and work with locals to help them improve their own development, its a win-win for everyone.

You can find locations that have established tech hubs or co-working spaces here:
www.techhub.com
coworker.com

You can also look into the cost and speed of the internet for many global locations here:
www.nomadlist.io

Create Your Own Job Wealth

As jobs are becoming harder to come by for graduates, why not create your own job opportunity by creating a business yourself? After all, you know your strengths, so why waste time trying to sell yourself to someone else?

Creating your own independent source of income can help generate a stable future for yourself. Put in the work now and you can make a future custom lifestyle possible. I would work 10 hours for myself to avoid working one hour for someone else. If you commit to making it happen, anything is possible.

After all, when you are your own boss you can play by your own rules. You can run with what works and you can experiment and improve yourself with what doesn't. All the time spent now building yourself up just makes you stronger and improves your personal development as well as your business.

Sure, there will be times when you have to make big decisions and wish for the safety net of job security, but it's all about taking risks for a better working environment for yourself. Like I said, if you fail, at least you tried, and you will learn so much from having been ambitious and pushed yourself to be a better person. it will be a great learning experience and that's what life is all about. Don't go through life knowing that you didn't at least give it a go, you would kick your future self.

If you have reached out to at least one individual you had never met before and possibly improved there life in some way, at least you have reached out to one individual and made a positive impact which might never have happened. Give it a thought, it's a big decision to make but it's one you should make on your own. Most importantly, if you're committed to the cause then that's all you can ask from yourself to gain the confidence in getting your idea out there.

If you have a great idea for a business, the world will be interested to see what you can offer, Show them what you can do and people might like what they see. Networking is key!

The way technology and the internet is growing, more and more people will learn about the digital nomad lifestyle and get a piece of it for themselves by moving into offering their skills as a freelancer instead of working at a big firm. They can charge the same rates, work remotely anywhere and follow their own rules, this is the joy of having a skill and getting more freedom from it.

Over in the US, surveys have shown that more people have started to shift from working in an office environment to working from home. It's both cost effective for the company and the employee can better focus on getting the work done.

In an office environment you have to work 9 to 5, at home you work until the day's tasks are complete, then you can get on with whatever you want to do once its finished, it suits everyone better.

The global work force is already adapting to remote working. Almost all jobs could be taken out of an office environment. Of course we will still need a work force for jobs such as police officers or fire fighters, but those that can be done online from almost anywhere will shift away from the office and may even be outsourced.

Becoming a Digital Nomad can pretty much be the same thing, just moving the work from the home, cutting out the home, car and house bills, o working remotely from the road where ever you can find wifi or a 3G connection.

If you want to see how easy it is to offer your skills online and find work from anyone who is willing to pay you, all you have to do is simply check freelance job search engines:
UpWork
Fiverr

Traditional Employment is Shifting

As freelancing grows, more business owners will seek to break away from the normal working life the world has followed for years. More creative ways of working will become apparent. This will affect employee numbers at firms and increase the need for freelancing individuals seeking to work more cost effectively.

If a company could cut out an expensive team and outsource the same work to a freelancer for a better price, what's stopping them?

What route will these companies take in the future? Who knows, but the employment landscape is changing. They will be open to creative ideas and freelancers could win over these companies as they can provide a more cost effective solution to get the job done. If the quality of work is not great then they will can just find another freelancer. The market is growing and the is enough choice for them to be selective.

Tuning your skills now to being the best in your field will help significantly in the future.

Established companies look to compete with competitors to stay alive. They will not just rely on their trusted work force because it's comfortable and works, they have to remain cost effective. Think about it, jobs in the traditional sense in the future will be a whole different ball game. Thinking differently as a freelancer might be a more realistic way to seek future secure employment.

I see endless possibilities beyond working as an intern for a company without pay, yet graduates still take this as it's the only option they can find. Working always looks good on your CV, so why don't you just work for yourself, get paid for it and build up your own reputation whilst travelling the world.

I'm not saying you can survive as a Digital Nomad forever, but you can look into the possibilities right now and see if it could work for you. When the time does come to stop globe trotting and you decide to settle, with all the experience you've picked up over the years you could create any number of opportunities in your chosen field. Anything is possible.

It's Never Been Easier to Start Your Own Business

It's all about building your own reputation, networking, gaining clients and building an audience. Become an expert in your own field and be great at it, if you can do this remotely for a few years, gain from this experience, and embrace the opportunity to travel, then doors will start to open.

In the past, it was difficult to start a business from scratch. You would first have to come up with an idea, next would be to source funding for your idea from bank or investors - next to impossible to get if without a great credit rating or valuable personally owned property.

If your idea was service based, you would need to be a leading expert or have a university degree in the subject. If it was product based, you would have to source well priced goods in your home country, which might be harder than you think, or search abroad where finding reliable suppliers is difficult and costly without good contacts.

Even then you might struggle to find an affordable work force, warehouse or distribution given that you have no reputation or built up trust in the industry.

Service based ideas would have been harder to establish as customer loyalty was dominated by companies going back generations. A new way of doing it was out of the question.

Today the tables have turned. Thanks to the internet it's never been easier to set up your own business and to be your own boss anywhere around the world. Local governments are even interested in financing great ideas for new entrepreneurs, as long as they have a good idea and a solid plan. Getting a loan to kick start your business idea has never been easier. Sure, employment with a company seems safer, but do you really want someone else running the show and gaining profit from your hard work?

Borders are no longer an issue for work; trade is truly global. You can code computer software in Thailand that you can sell to a Brazilian, create a new product on CAD and outsource it to a factory in China using Alibaba.com, program a video game in Norway to play on a smart phone which you can sell around the world using an app store, write a book in your student dorm in Holland to sell to a global ebook market. The web has no borders and it's up to you to seek out the opportunities and make the most out of it. If you don't do it, someone else will.

Ways to earn money online

There are many ways to make money online to support a location independent lifestyle. You just have to think outside of the box and think what work can be done whilst remaining mobile, online and with tools that you can carry in your hand luggage.

Here are some examples:

• Web Designer
• Web Developer
• Graphic Designer
• Animator
• Copywriter
• Illustrator
• Usability Tester
• SEO Consultant
• Mobile Applications Designer
• Mobile Applications Development
• Dropshipper
• Logo Designer
• Book Cover Designer
• Proofreader
• Photographer
• Translator
• Journalist
• Market Strategist

- Email Marketer
- Accountant
- Motivational Coach
- Virtual Assistant
- E-book Writer
- Marketing consultant
- Press Release Writer
- Project Manager
- Resume Writer
- Voice recording Artist
- Technical Support Specialist
- Video Editor
- Web Content Writer
- Website Translator
- Stock Photographer
- Legal Advisor
- Game Developer
- Travel Writer
- Online Game Player/Tester

The list is endless. Many jobs can be done remotely with only a laptop and an internet connection. Does it make you wonder why you would want to be fixed in one location when you could be mobile with your profession?

Look at the list and see what areas appeal to you or what you are already good at. Spend a couple of days looking around Google, YouTube or Udemy at those areas of interest. You will find numerous free tutorials by others doing those professions online and explaining step-by-step how to do it.

Do Your Homework

Never invest in something without doing your research first. It can be tempting to buy into courses and workshops at an early stage, but it could well be best to try and make some money first before investing in courses. Sure, you may come across something that could propel you faster into the field you want to move into, but proper investment, both of your time and money, is just as important when building a new lifestyle.

Later on, as you progress with your online business, you might not even want to take the course after all. If you're making a profit and still think the course can provide value, then go for it, but do hold back from impulse purchases. You should spend time with an online course not just chuck cash at it in the hope that you will excel faster. There is no such thing as a magic bullet, and the course may not work.

Ebooks are helpful as they can condense resources, which you might have spent hours or days finding online, into one convenient place. Its a good idea to invest in cheap ebooks if they come highly recommended.

Invest £100 & Kickstart Your Business

From the start you should set yourself a test investment limit. It's a small amount to commit to and might save you a lot in the long run. £100 is a realistic amount to invest into a passion project. Use this funding from your own pocket and use it to create the foundation of your new business venture.

You can create a business for this amount very easily, but you shouldn't commit much more finance than this at the start. If you try and things don't work out, then losing this amount is not a massive punch in the face, but it will allow you to test something out and give it a go.

This small amount will teach you to be frugal with your finances and find solutions that are more cost effective. Rather than chucking all the money you have into one pot, you can seek free alternatives that do the same job without committing yourself too much. Later on in the journey, once you've started to make some money, you can invest it back into your business to keep growing. Every time you stumble across costs or investments that you feel could improve your business, just add this to a comeback later list. When you have generated more income, you can decide whether it's worth reinvesting your profits towards these tools. This way you will never waste money.

A lot of information and tools can be found on the web for free, yes that's right, free. Sure, it might not be the ideal method, but if it works and you can keep your financial commitment low at the start, it gives you a change to see if this lifestyle is possible for you.

What to do with your £100 Investment

Buy a server spot, make some business cards, register a domain, buy a cheap WordPress theme and pay a designer to create a logo for you.

All the above can be easily done for under £100. There you go, you have yourself a business.

Why a domain and server? It's a small investment, but makes you stand out as more professional. Taking the step to do this shows that you mean business and you're in it for the long run. You can create a free email address with gmail using your new URL. My email is: dave@traveldave.co.uk, it comes across as more professional and trustworthy than a hotmail account.

A domain and host can be purchased with a one click Wordpress install that is easy to use and set up. You can check out host companies that offer an easy to install Wordpress host service such as SiteGround. This is perfect If you're not technical and require some initial support to get the site up and running, but is still low cost.

You can create a free Wordpress account that comes with its own URL, but purchasing your own unique domain will make you stand out amongst the market. When people visit your site they will instantly assume you are a trustworthy and authentic source.

You can be very successful without taking this route, but the WordPress.org free alternative does come with limitations that restrict what you can do with sponsors on your site.

Registering your domain is really important as this will become your business. I use 123-Reg to look up available domain names, you should go for a .com, .co or .org account. If your audience is location specific then a .ca or .co.uk site could work for you instead. This is when you will discover if your business name has already taken. If the domain is not available, you may wish to reconsider the name - having the correct domain is just that important.

Once you have registered your domain, it's yours and you can begin to build yourself up. All the time and effort you put into this site becomes your portfolio, your art gallery, your shop front and your identity.

Why WordPress? It's simple, easy to use and fun. If you have coding skills, then great, build your own site. If you don't have the coding skills, don't let this dissuade you from achieving your goals. Armed with the internet, it's very easy to find endless amounts of forums with answers to any of your WordPress questions. With time it's easy to find solutions to any

WordPress problems. Sure, there are many other blogging platforms you can also use, but I have found registering a domain and setting up a server easy to do with Wordpress from the start, and coding/setup solutions are easy to find if you're internet smart.

Should you buy a theme? You can search for free Wordpress themes, with hundreds of options available. If you find a theme that works for you, then perfect, use it. Free themes are a good idea at the start if you want your £100 investment to go further. Do also have a look into the paid options for nicer site designs, normally you can find great themes for as little as €20-30 that will make your blog look more unique and attractive. Have a look at woothemes.com, for examples. The problem with free themes is you that you might bump into problems and things to tweak that aren't easily dealt with. Paid themes tend to have more support and forums with questions and answers surrounding various issues and alterations for the theme you have chosen. Paying a little can go a long way in terms of making things less complicated, but if you're lucky enough to find a free theme that suits your purpose, then why not go for it.

Check out woothemes.com to have a look at, easy to install WordPress themes on offer for low prices, backed up with a great support team.

However, you should be careful as you will find incredible designs with a high price tag. At the starting stage I suggest you build an audience first before blowing money on a top site layout. There is no need to have a great looking site with no content, as it can be misleading. Later, once your blog starts to gain stable traffic and builds a following, you might want to give your site a new design, but it isn't necessary until then. Don't chuck your hard earned cash away in the hope that it will bring a return on investment; get the community first, then look into this later. It is worthwhile collecting feedback on what your community wants to see from your new site so that the investment is worthwhile. Big design changes and improvements will have a dramatic positive impact on your community.

Don't pay to shine your shoes until you need to impress. Impress when its right, then expectations will grow, rather than drop, from the start.

Investing in your logo can make it stand out more. If you're a wizard with photoshop then go for it, design your own logo. If you have no clue what you are doing, pay an expert to do what they do best. It doesn't have to be expensive, but this little investment can go a long way. Your logo, just like your domain and site, should be everything you stand for, you should be proud of it and this will motivate you to do what you do. First, ask friends who are knowledgable in this area, they might even create one for you in exchange for a crate of beer! If you want to be more specific with what you want, then you may not wish to ask a friend. However, a little cash can go a long way in this area.

A good price for a well designed log would be in the region of £20-40. You can find designers online such as my friend Tom @TOMINC who designed my site, logo and even this eBook cover. Normally, they have portfolios of logos that they have created for companies in the past and you can get a better picture of what is possible. You can also visit sites that have a bidding platform and designers can bid for your work so that you have more options.

Alternatively, you can use fiverr.com to locate designers that are willing to design logos for $5 (a fiver!) Just change the search to order their listings by most popular or highest rated to locate the best logo designers.

It is really important that your logo hits the nail on the head regarding what your business is all about. To be a great design, it has to stand out, represent you as a brand, relate to your business, and not be overly complicated or cluttered. Just make sure that it's memorable, makes sense and stands out and you'll be on to a winner. Creating a great logo for your business will help boost confidence and give you something to represent in the future. Try not to cut corners with this.

Business cards? These are great for networking. You're going to bump into a lot of people and you will want to talk about your business. Talking is one thing, but giving someone contact details that they can follow up on will increase the chance that they do. If you were just talk to them and hand them nothing to follow up with, they might simply forget you. I suggest business cards from the start because they are very inexpensive. You can use vistaprint.com to create a free business card theme and just pay for postage. It doesn't have to be fancy, just show people what you can offer and how they can get in touch with you, then you can attract the right people at the right time.

You can purchase more upmarket, yet affordable, professional business cards from moo.com if you still have some of your investment remaining and want to improve your first impression.

At the Start, Free is Always Better

Wasting money when you don't have it can be the biggest mistake from the start. I made this mistake and got into a lot of trouble over it. You want your business to be successful and you will do whatever it takes to make it happen, just make sure this passion is invested with time and not money, you have to remain frugal. Sure an expensive Canon DSLR camera will create better videos for your YouTube channel, but if no one is watching them, then why do they have to be of such amazing quality? Use a camera phone, which you probably already have in your pocket, and utilize the tools you already own to create and generate an audience first before investing in high-end equipment.

Sure, it will improve the quality of your output, but you first must earn the money or traffic to justify sacrificing money on such high-risk items. Overspending could damage everything you have worked towards, and money could be better spent in other areas that need the investment more.

One mistake I made was to pay Facebook to promote a post on my "like" page to get higher traffic; it was a complete waste of money. People who want to read your content will be able to find it if they really want to, you shouldn't spend money pushing content to people that don't want to read it in the first place. Don't take short cuts with your cash in order to create a higher gain. It just won't happen, be patient, be happy with the people you have attracted from the start, seek free alternatives to improve this growth, then you can start experimenting with paid traffic builders when you're in the right position, not when you are still starting out, tempting though it sounds.

Free is always best at the start; create, build and embrace the journey getting to where you want to be. Once you're making a profit, invest in areas that will help the journey but not until you're in the best position to make those choices. This will ensure that your business grows with you build this new venture.

You can get started for as little as £100 easily. Once your first venture is going well and making a profit, you can invest another £100 into a new venture and start again.

This it the general idea of being successful in business - not putting all your eggs into one basket and maximising your investment. A small investment is a small risk. Some ideas will be successful, and others will fail, and you will learn a lot on either journey. However, by only investing £100, you won't be kicking yourself if it fails, making it easier to just pick yourself up and try again.

It Will Take Time to Establish Yourself

It's next to impossible to become an overnight sensation. You will need to build up trust and encourage others that you are a valued source. This skill takes time to learn, but if you remain committed to your cause, then others will be committed to follow.

Trust is the most valuable quality that you will need to build with your audience. If you are not a trusted source then why would people buy into what you offer? If you offer something of value and have great communication with your clients & followers they will continue to support you and be happy to look into everything you do.

You might have a unique way of playing the piano and become a massive viral sensation overnight on YouTube, but still you need to work out how to manage this new audience that's coming your way and keep them interested.

From a distance you have been fast-tracked an audience, you're still the same person as you were yesterday, only your audience has grown.

The majority of YouTube sensations have actually built up an decent audience prior to a big viral hit and know how to manage their audience. The audience has only grown in number, but the value they offer to their new followers will still remain the same and will continue to grow.

That person is unlikely to have just picked up the piano the day before, got on YouTube the next day and made that happen.

They most probably have been playing the piano for many years, perfecting their craft and earned their viral hit. You don't just become big overnight, it's a formula that can be followed that you have to dedicate yourself to over time.

You will have to build yourself from the ground up. It's not as fun as you might picture it to be. Don't assume there'll be instant success, as it's likely to be a long road ahead. The quicker you learn and accept this fact, the better.

At the start you will create great content and products, but won't see the traffic you desire. That's why it's so important to build an audience following a slower organic growth model (known as "long tail").

You may have a small audience to start with, such as your family and friends. Be sure to get the most out of this. Make a great impact on your early followers and treat them as if you are being followed by millions.

Why? People that have followed from the start will believe in you no matter what. Learn from this experience and it will help you in the future when your business grows. When you start to gain more loyal followers you will already know what to do.

As your audience grows, more and more people will discover your great content that has built up over time.

The time you put in during the early stages will help you to learn what works and what doesn't through trial and error stages. It's best to do this through an audience you know personally, so that the feedback received is better, and will be able to prepare you for the future.

Make it personal. Personality is key, and if people like who you are, they will like what you are about, what you stand for and support what you're trying to achieve.

The web is full of generic content, but if there is a face behind yours and the audience share your values, then you are capturing a unique audience that wants to buy what you are offering.

Trust + personality = a unique audience that will want to jump aboard the ship you're sailing.

Research your market

Before you start your journey look into who is already covering your field, most probably there are already experts out there doing what you want to do and that share your passion and creativity.

To discover who these people are, all it takes is one simple Google search. Open the top 20 into tabs and look at their sites to find out what the experts are doing, what you should do, as well as what you find the most appealing and why.

You might even stumble across blog posts related to a selection of top blogs in the field you're researching that someone recommended.

Follow these blogs and their YouTube/Twitter/ Facebook feed and learn from them by surrounding yourself with their content. This will provide a massive source of information for you to discover. Follow them, subscribe to their podcasts and join their RSS feeds (I recommend using bloglovin.com for this).

Look around their blogs, see what they do to attract new sign ups, how they interact with their audience, sell products and deliver content over time. Learn how they get their content to you and adapt the areas you like the most or find most effective to your future plans.

Make them your main source of encouragement and influence. If they are able to do it, then why can't you? Comment on their blogs, engage with them and reach out to them when possible.

By engaging with their content, you will learn a lot about their process of delivering content to their community and you can adapt these methods to your own business. The web is all about learning and sharing content, their might even be ebooks to help you with your specific field. Many others have already been doing what you want to do for many years and can offer a lot of knowledge, insight and experience.

By cutting out everything else and focusing on these influences, it will encourage you to achieve your goal. Most likely they are nice people and happy to reach out to others who want to do the same as them. They most probably have also surrounded themselves with people they also believe in, and by creating support units everyone can encourage each other to complete goals.

The web can be a crowded place, so focus on around 10 bloggers that best cover your field of business, which is a manageable amount of people to follow around your niche market. If you focus all your time on this limited amount of space, it's more beneficial. If your interests or influences change, then these 10 can be altered over time.

Follow news channels that report on your industry to keep up to date with growing trends and emerging markets. You can also follow them on Twitter or place them in your RSS feed. You can join forums, or support groups on Facebook and Reddit, for further help and advice, surrounding yourself in communities where people are following the same path.

If you discover that others are able make a living through these skills, then it's great encouragement for you to complete your goals. It's very important to test the water before you swim so that you know whether to get in or not.

If you are finding it hard to discover others working online in your niche, then you are either onto a winner or there might be a good reason why no one is in your niche market. Look into those that might have failed and discover why this happened. Maybe you'll be able to work out why it was not successful and turn it into a winner.

Invest your time and experiment. You might want to quit your job and poor everything into your passion to make it happen. I suggest not to do this. You could be making a big mistake and that's why research is very important to assess the possibilities from the start.

Looking around the web and following others that are doing what you want to do can help to build your confidence. Research is free and only requires your time. The concept here is to start looking, see if your ideas are viable and surround yourself with the correct advice. Then you can see if you want to take the next step towards becoming a digital nomad.

Creating an Audience

When you gain a circle of interested followers enjoying your content, they will engage and share, enabling further audience growth. Think of them as your sales team, a team that is willing to share your story without you even putting any effort in at all, isn't that great!

I love getting messages from my personal friends saying "Hey Dave! You're the travel dude, I read one of your blogs and told my friend who is going travelling all about your blog and they want to find out more". This small 20 second message on Facebook has shown me that at some point during a pub conversation, when travel was raised, I was the first person they thought of and it lead to this Facebook message.

When you hear your message is being spread by a friend, an element of vouching has taken place. If your friend can recommended your service or product without even having been asked, then you are probably already doing a great job and your concept is easy for an audience to be attracted to and share.

A friend that has vouched for you to there own personal circle is on board with your venture. They have already built up trust with you as a person without you even talking to them directly. This is exactly what you want to achieve when building an audience, creating a product that has a solution to a problem that many people share and will recommend to others. Natural content sharing is the best form of sharing and if you can achieve this you're going down the right path.

I got most of my first traffic from people I have never personally met through friends telling other friends about my travel blog. They knew that I was a mutual friend, establishing immediate trust. This was one of the most difficult elements to achieve on the web with lots of competition. But by doing a great job and being vouched for by friends means that you have something worth sharing.

This is one of the most powerful ways to build up a larger audience. Build an audience around friends and associates, and let them share your story. If they don't want to spread your venture, then it's going to be a difficult to get an audience outside of your close friendship circle.

It's not easy to get 1,000 followers overnight, but you should definitely set yourself a timeframe to work towards that goal. Remember that figures only look good on paper, make sure that you can use this to attract advertisers. However, from the start you should focus on building a loyal following rather than treating them as figures in a spreadsheet.

Think about it, would you rather have a genuine audience of 546 enthusiast climbers following your Facebook page related to climbing products, or 3,000 random members of the general public? Don't focus on building figures, focus on growth that attracts the correct target audience, naturally. If you have a great product, present yourself in the best way possible and make it easily shared, then the audience will gradually come over time. There's no need to rush this process.

Communication is Key

Every message you receive, be it via Facebook, email, Twitter or a comment section, you should take the opportunity to engage and improve the trust and value you have with your audience. Sure, you might get very long messages, but these people have sought you out over anyone else. You should reply with great advice, which will encourage them to become a loyal follower. Never ignore messages, it's so important to engage with your audience on a personal level to make bonds and to spread your message. At first this will be time consuming, but over time, as your audience grows and you start to get more responses, you will start to move towards a natural auto response. This gets easier over time, so practice at the beginning to become better at it.

First you should connect with those you already have around you. At the start you can create an audience amongst your personal circle. From the start you will most probably have an audience of two, your Mum and Dad, they are the easiest sell to follow you, but soon this grows into around 200 when you tell your Facebook friends, then if 200 each tell two of their close friends, you have established an audience of 600. When the outside world see 600 people are interested in you, then your audience can grow quickly to 2,000. At this point you become an established source in your area, allowing growth towards five figures.

You get the picture, but this takes time to establish, Over time your audience will grow and popularity will increase as you start to gain trust. It's better to grow organically than overnight so you can learn how to manage a changing audience size over time. If this was to all happen at once, you might buckle under pressure and misuse the opportunity.

If the first 200 people won't even engage with what you want to offer, then you have a tough time ahead. They know you in a personal way and their criticism is easier to take as they will give it to you in a friendly way.

You should seek out and appreciate criticism from friends and family, it should be seen as a positive experience as it can only help you improve. Take on board what they have said and work towards improving yourself. Those that are close to you will be more honest with you. They are your audience, and the advice they give might be harsh, but in most cases they will be right to point out what you are doing wrong. Not all feedback is useful, but use your own judgement and thank them for their feedback. If they give you advice it is generally because they want to help you. You could even ask them if they wouldn't mind helping you out to solve the problem, they might be willing to help.

This support network of early adopters will be a big help when you start out, and will support you through the beginning, and be your biggest promoters as you grow and improve. Nurture them, and use their advice wisely on your journey!

If it's not working out, reach out to them for advice. This may help you solve issues faster. Aim to act on on the criticisms that you receive, this is great at the start; it's never too early, or too late, to make changes.

Working on capturing and nurturing your first audience will help you in the future to build trust with others you don't already know.

Building up an audience in this way will is time consuming but valuable. You will have times when what you are doing won't work as well as you would like, just be patient and your time will eventually come.

In order to make sure you are able to allow yourself to grow you should capture your audience. When someone visits your site, they will leave at some point, will they come back? Who knows, but one thing is for sure and that is you can set up capturing techniques to keep them within your community.

They say it takes up to 7 interactions for someone online to buy a product, that's why it's important to keep them within your community longer or they will visit your site once and never return. By keeping them around you have more of a chance to turn this community interaction into a sale.

Importance of an Email List

The number one thing you should have on your site from day one is an email list sign-up form. Either through a box on your blog page, or a pop-up, this allows them to opt in to more when they like what they read. They may visit your site and think you're awesome, but as soon as they click away to another website and you risk being forgotten, maybe forever.

Keep offering them great content and they will continue to follow. You have to remember that when you go to your own web browser you have blogs and websites that you like to follow, these are relationships that have been built up over time and give you an incentive or need to revisit them.

People stop following some websites over time for a number of reasons, but think - what keeps you going back to the same websites everyday? You will get something out of it, and for that reason the web is a very competitive. If you're able to offer something of unique interest in a unique way then you will be get returning visitors.

It might be the style in which you write, your humour, or the information you provide that keeps them coming back for more. That's why an email list is very important, you capture an audience that will keep engaging with you as long as the content you offer is of value. An email list is something you can begin at the start that will grow with you.

Over time you can use this helpful list to sell products, launch new ideas and keep everyone up to date with what you do. Without this list, it's much harder to keep them interested as you need a channel to remind them to keep coming back, which rarely happens without some sort of subscription.

If people find you through a search engine, they will generally leave again very quickly, but if you can bring them onboard the ride, you're on to a winner. In most cases, if they enjoyed what they got out of visiting your site they will be happy to receive more. An email list is one of the best ways to capture this continued support.

Some followers might opt out of your email list over time, but the large majority will stay put so that this useful resource will come in handy for product announcements or launches.

I use MailChimp for my mailing list, you use this service for up to 2,000 subscribers for free and it allows you to create wonderful templates to send to your followers.

I like to use a Wordpress Plugin called Thrive Lead, which creates pop-up and email subscription forms for your site and measures the conversion rates per visitor so that you can perform A/B testing on what works most effectively on your site.

It's also a great idea to create free giveaways for those who sign up to your email list, this further encourages them to take up a subscription.

Use Analytics From the Start

If you have no way of measuring your traffic, then you are pretty much communicating blind. You need to measure all areas of your traffic in order to learn about what is working or not working and how best to tweak your business in order to have lasting positive effects.

First of all, you want to make sure that you have authorised your site with Google. This is done by placing some code into your site header that allows Google to can scan your site and sync with Google analytics. This code, and information on how to install it can be easily found in Google's webmaster tools.

Best of all its completely free to upload your website to Google analytics and you can download free Google apps to your phone that monitor your daily stats. You can easily fall into the trap of checking it every hour as it's interesting to see whats happening on your site, but try to avoid this as you will be wasting a lot of time. It's best to check every few days or to schedule a weekly spot-check. I like to use the Jetpack dashboard plugin for WordPress to keep an eye on my analytics daily from the login page.

The information you will want to know includes where people are visiting from, which device they look at your site on, which web browsers they use, what keywords they have searched to find you, how long they stayed on each page, which pages they went to, from which website did they come from to yours.

All this information is useful for discovering the performance of your website and to work out how it can be improved. For example, if you notice that people are visiting your site from Pinterest a lot, engage in Pinterest a little more compared with, say, a Google+ page that is getting no traffic at all, or alternatively build more on Google+ to improve the traffic coming from that source.

You may notice that, for example, Dutch people are reading your blog more often. In this case it is a good idea to try and aim your content more towards popular Dutch websites. You may notice that some people are only visiting one of your pages for 2 seconds, so not really engaging at all, maybe you should delete that page or improve it so that readers engage with it more.

Maybe your site is being viewed more on mobile devices than on laptops, so maybe you should run tests to make sure that your website looks great on mobile devices. There are so many ways you can use analytics, it's such a helpful set of tools for improving the performance of your content and help you better engage with people in the future. No longer will you be in the dark, you will be able to clearly see where things are going right or wrong.

You will also learn that different audiences come from different platforms; not all will come from the same place. Therefore it is key to branch out your content in multiple unique ways to capture yourself a wider audience.

Creating content to engage an audience

Creating content can be a great way to get your business across to the masses. It allows you to documents the journey you're taking and can help to promote the products that you're working on. Creating content such as videos, photos, podcasts, or blog posts keeps your audience engaged with what you have to offer. Simply creating a static page that never changes will struggle to draw in an audience, while creating regular new content with a schedule gives everyone a reason to come back and see what you've been up to.

Passive content is great. Every piece you create only needs to be created once and then it's on the web forever - just think about that. When you work in a factory you just do the same thing over and over again, starting again every time. However, when you create online content, once its posted, its on the web and you will never have to re-write the same blog post, take the same photo, or compose the same tweet ever again.

Sure, you might have to go back to some posts and edit or update them, but mostly if you put in the effort first time now you are building a portfolio, you are establishing your presence on the web and you can keep on adding and building on what you create. At the start it might feel empty, but everyone has to begin from somewhere. Just don't worry, never give up and keep creating content that people want to consume and enjoy.

Get it out there, don't worry about it being perfect, otherwise you might end up spending a lifetime writing your first post. I'm serious - just get it out there. Perfectionism is one of the biggest rookie mistakes in blogging. Of course, you don't want to post rubbish, but half the mountain climb is just getting your content out there quick enough to leave footprints on the web and to engage your audience.

For videos, you will need to learn the process of editing and publishing content. At the start people will offer advice on how to improve your posts as they will spot mistakes in your work. It's always best to notice these issues during the early stages than later on. Mistakes happen, it's all part of the learning process. Get content out there and grow with your audience.

Quality over quantity? Yes. Rubbish is bad, why would anyone read it? Just read it yourself and ask yourself, would you be entertained by this post? If you think the answer is yes then it's probably good enough. Set yourself guidelines such as 600 to 800 words per blog post and just experiment with what works.

Keep it short and sweet, then you know at least your readers will read until the end to establish an opinion. The last thing you want is readers going off your blog completely and not finishing the post, it should be engaging enough that they get to the end of the post.

You should not be afraid to give opinions within your posts. You don't have to remain neutral within your blog posts, otherwise it can come across as too robotic and disingenuous. If your post doesn't feel real they will stop reading, why would anyone want to read posts that don't feel honest?

Make sure your content is related to your product. Going off on a tangent and talking about completely unrelated subjects will confuse your readers and won't make sense. If you really want to write about an entirely different subject feel free to set up a private blog for fun to write these sort or articles. It's just important to make sure your main blog doesn't lose focus. This is the same for Facebook and Twitter, keep two accounts, one for business and one for personal, so that you can share the correct content on the channel that it best fits.

People will come to your post looking for your opinion, so write what you truly think. Create content that will attract comments, and make them want to share it with friends on Facebook and Twitter. It doesn't have to be offensive, just engaging enough for the reader to want more content you create. We all have different styles and tastes, if you're able to attract an audience that likes your unique take on a subject. then you can build an audience around this.

If this results in negative comments, then at least you have sparked a debate and generated traffic and interest from other readers. Make sure you don't delete comments because it negatively effects your post ranking. Instead, take it on board as feedback. You can either let another member of your community respond and make room for a debate, or you can add an honest response to the comment. Deleting a comment because you don't agree is not a great move, unless it's abusive of course. If you noticed your blog is getting a lot of spammy comments, don't worry, you can simply install a Wordpress app called Akismet, it's free and does a great job at stopping spam robots posting comments on your blog.

Write your own personality. People don't just want facts or filler, they seek entertainment. With so many blogs and so much information to consume on the web, appreciate that these people are visiting your site. Normally people choose to read a blog either because they value the information given or they enjoy the style in which it is written. Either write in a way that's easy to follow or write in a way that makes them want to keep reading.

Lay out your text out so it can be followed easily. Avoid writing a novel, write so there eyes don't leave the page and they can bounce to each line easily. This is important because reading on computers is different to reading on an e-reader or a real book, they can easily lose momentum and disappear to another website.

However, there is nothing wrong with writing and crafting a long form article if the information is in depth and useful to the reader. Some of my longer posts are about how to deal with complex situations that need a lot of explanation. If you are able to write an article like this, that is crammed full of useful information, then there is no problem with that. I've found that doing one of these posts once a month generates and creates a lot of value for readers. However, breaking such an article into five articles in a series is also another way of going about this. Just do what works best for you and your readers.

Write small clusters of text, not massive paragraphs. If words do not need to be there, then delete them. Use bold text and italics to highlight important sections and phrases. Also have bright colours for URL Links and try and highlight big words or words of importance that will make readers jump to the next line. Ask a question that sums up the whole blog at the end so that readers are encouraged naturally to comment on the blog post. This helps with regards to engaging readers and encourages them to visit your other posts and come back to your blog in the future.

Offer something of value to keep them hooked. If you're writing for the sake of writing, then you're going to lose out. People want entertainment and you have to offer this. It could either be something they can relate to, something they can agree or disagree with, or some sort of useful information that they wish to seek. Telling personal stories of your experience by adding a personal touch works as well. Trying to share unique insights into your story to help create a connection and trust between you and the reader.

If readers get entertainment or useful information from you then they will value what you have created. Then they will be encouraged to stick with you on your journey.

SEO & keywords

If you become best friends with Google, it will gradually boost your site traffic for you. Use keywords in your title and posts to help search engines, such as Google, to match your blog to what people are searching for.

Compare the two post titles: "How to stream online content abroad, best of all it's free" vs. "Lets watch something fun on the road". People searching for this kind of information would probably Google "Watch online content abroad for free". In this instance it is clear that the first post title is much better than the latter. You can gain new visitors to your blog by using keywords in your blog posts to help search engines easily match your blog posts with what people are searching for.

The best way to approach titles is to simply do a search for similar blog posts and look at the keywords that the search engine suggests. When you type in one word, Google normally gives you 10 instant suggestions for what you might be looking for. These suggestions are popular searches that get a lot of hits. Balance and shape your title to fit these as best as you can, dependent on the subject of course.

It's best to already have the title created before you craft your post so that you know which words to use within the blog text in order to help boost where your blog post appears in search engine results.

Once you have incorporated the keywords into the title, try to add a bonus golden nugget at the end of the post title. In the above suggestion, I added "it's free". Free things are always popular, and common search targets, so that's an added bonus. Generally, you want to add something extra to make people want to click for example:

"Travel Dave's Top 5 Travel tips, I wonder if you dare to do tip 4?"

What I added to the end of a popular title is an extra segment that draws the reader in. They will really want to find out what I suggested for tip 4. It really draws attention and I'm sure you've read similar links on Facebook before. Maybe add a cropped photo that does not reveal what the title is talking about. Readers are drawn towards limited teasers and want to find out what the fuss is all about. It's entertaining for them, creates excitement and they will read the whole post to come reach the conclusion.

SEO (Search Engine Optimisation) is the art of writing your blog post to allow search engines to assess if the person using their search engine would find your page relevant or not. Adding keywords in your post, as well as the title, will boost your post on search engines and generates more traffic, and most importantly, new readers. This allows more readers to find your blog for the first time, find the post enjoyable, scan around the rest of your blog, like the other posts, enjoy the design, brand and image, and then opt into following you in the future. It's the perfect way to capture new audiences and reach out to new readers not in your current social circle.

Make sure you don't game the system. Creating popular keyword titles and putting words in your post frequently that have no relation to your site or the topic matter will make readers leave your site straight away. The more times that this happens, the higher your bounce rate will get.

This is why its important to either create short, easy to read content, so that readers don't leave straight away, or alternatively, long informative posts that keep readers engaged to stick around and then maybe click on another post on your blog.

To discover which keywords are popular you could use Google keywords planner, here you can search for what keywords are of a high or low value and then work out how many hits these keywords get. Then you can work out which areas need covering or not.

Just be careful - never write a post just for SEO! Instead, write quality posts that adapt to the necessary SEO. This is important as avoids losing focus on what you set out to achieve. Remember you will already have an audience that seeks great content from you, so don't damage the relationship you already have in order to gain more by selling out, readers will see through this and stop following you, which is bad news.

This is the same for selling products in your post via links. Make sure that what you're pushing is beneficial to the reader, don't post them for the sake of posting and only share links to websites or products you actually use personally. Then, when you are talking about them it comes across as completely natural to the reader. Only recommend what you believe in so that your readers can believe in them, too.

You should use links in posts to help solve problems that you explain in the post - these links point to the solutions. This is a good way of sharing links, not just for the sake of sharing links, which google hates and picks up on. They can delete your page from the search results altogether if you continue to abuse this trust. Be careful with back links and avoid this happening to you.

If you can relate a past post to your current post, link the two blog posts together with a back link to the other post you have already written. This link will keep readers on your site to and help them to delve further into your other content.

You can install a free Wordpress plug-in called "Wordpress SEO by Yoast" to help improve SEO to your site.

Having an easy-to-find URL helps too. Built into Wordpress is a feature that allows your blog title to be the URL of the blog post. You should always do this, as it helps search engines to find your post more easily and boost traffic to your blog post. It's an easy trick to follow so you have no excuse!

Example:

traveldave.co.uk/book-cheaper-flights/

vs.

http://traveldave.co.uk/124ftr432

Search engines prefer the first one. It's both easier to find and clearer to readers when they read and share it. This will help boost your SEO rating.

Image is Everything

Pictures tell a thousand words. It's easier to show readers what you mean through photos than in a paragraph of writing. Visual content is always rewarding and if placed correctly, can be massively effective.

Make sure your pictures are of high quality and that you either own the rights, or have permission to use them. You can get in a lot of trouble by posting other peoples pictures on your site and passing them off as your own. Simply ask the photographer if you can use their photos and make sure you credit every photo you use. The best solution is to either use your own photographs or to seek out a picture stock site to use on your website, such as istockphoto.com.

Just make sure that the photos do not look like they have been purchased to use in an advertising campaign.

People want to see you in the picture, so be creative. As often as I can, I try to place a picture of me as the main photo in the blog post. Every blog post should have a banner picture that relates to the title and ties into the content so it all makes sense. If the image doesn't relate to what you wrote, it could damage the quality of the blog post and potentially confuse or mislead your readers.

In addition, if the picture is of poor quality it will reflect badly on you, so make sure it's edited and cropped well to showcase your blog post in a great way. Try and make a screen shot of your photo to take the image size down. If a picture file size is too large it might slow down your page loading time. Making the page more static will allow images to load more quickly without affecting the quality. You can also host your pictures off-site so that they load quicker. I host and store my photos on Flickr, where it is really easy to grab the coding and embed the picture in a blog post.

Try to not smother your blog post with too many pictures. You don't want to drown out the text unless the blog is about photos taken on a particular subject or recent trip. Make sure the images are not too large and that they fit nicely around the text layout for optimal presentation.

If you can add a video to help explain a subject, then this is also a good tip. People enjoying watching content online, if you can create a video on a subject then this is another great to get into. I can be more tricky and time-consuming to create and edit videos, but if done correctly, they can be hugely rewarding and generate a lot of traffic.

Creating a Schedule

You want to stick to a manageable blog schedule that both you and your readers can follow. I have stopped following blogs before because they posted 5 blogs a day and most people just don't have the time or inclination to read that much content.

Working out a blog post timeframe balance is tricky and it is best decide by measuring your reader interaction. You can do this by experimenting with schedules and measuring your traffic with google analytics. From the start you want to set yourself high content targets just to make your site look full and busy - one blog a week will not cut at the start. If your blog has only 3 posts, it will like readers walking into an empty shop. Getting your first blog posts out there helps to build your audience.

From the start you can set yourself a realistic goal of writing one blog post a day for one month. This means that after one month you would have had the chance to play around with the information I posted above, learn the ropes and look into the problems you stumbled across, as well as filling up your blog with great content.

Just like buying a new pair of hiking boots, you want to walk around in them for a while to wear them in. The same goes for a blog - setting a goal of completing 30 blogs in one month is both achievable and will train you for the demands of a blogging routine.

After your set goal is completed, you can look at the traffic over the month. Which days and times were most popular for visitors? What were they looking for on your blog? Which posts worked and which didn't? You can see where all of your visitors come from and which search engines display your posts. Then, after a month, you will be more confident with testing the water and can work with what you've learned.

Try different styles of blog posts and see what works best to engage your audience. Some examples of blog posts are:

• Reviews
• Answering a question
• List posts (e.g. top 5 places to visit in Singapore)
• Telling a personal story
• Asking a Question
• Useful tips
• Link Posts
• Interviews

As an example, I post two blog posts per week. This is a manageable schedule for me and it gets an optimum amount of traffic from my readers as its not too much or too little content. I can then be selective with my posts, discover new subjects to blog about over the week and then write a solid article.

Make sure you have a system to make notes on your blog ideas. One might pop in your head while just walking around and you don't want to lose it. Having a blog idea section on your to-do list helps when you have run out of other creative ideas. If I see something that could be interesting to blog about later I just take a picture of it to come back to it later. This ensures you will never forget.

Another great idea when thinking of subjects to blog about is simply to have a look at other bloggers pages for inspiration. You can add your own personal spin to a subject they've written about, or get ideas for how to write about subjects you have on your list.

Another area you can blog about is popular news events that relate to your field. If you can blog about a particular angle that's not been covered, this can bring in big traffic. This has happened to me in the past on a few subjects.

Make sure you never publish your work until you have proofread your article a number of times. You should make sure everything is in order within the preview before its published to the world. Preview in Wordpress lets you check the post as if it's live on the web before publishing so that you can check everything is working.

In the preview you want to open all the links and make sure they are directed to the correct page.

Check any embedded code such as photos to make sure they can be viewed and come are the correct size and layout. Check the font size, text layout and formatting as well.

For spellchecking I use a built in app called Ginger, which is an advanced spell checker. Trust me, I need to use this a lot. Make sure you read your post once more and don't be lazy about it. If you don't want to read it, then why would your readers?

Then take a step back and check it the overall post, make sure it looks appealing and easy to follow - it should look like a masterpiece! Then when you click publish you can be confident and proud of your blog post, and be happy to push it to the world on your social media platforms.

It takes between 2-3 hours to plan, craft, write, add titles and links, and perform a final check, before publishing a blog post. Over time, this process will become quicker and easier as you gain more experience.

BlogLovin and Feedly seem to be the new RSS feeds of choice, so make sure your audience is aware that they can read your content on these channels by providing plugins to easily add your blog to their feed.

You can also plug your RSS feed into a weekly summary email that can be sent out to all of your readers within MailChimp. This process can be automated so that your readers will always be updated with your posts without any extra effort on your part.

You can also install a sharing plugin at the end of the blog so that readers can share a piece easily once its read via their social media platforms, this is great for growing your audience outside your closed circle.

Make sure that your audience gets the content at the right time or you might lose their traffic altogether. It would be a shame to write a great piece and have no one read it, especially when you put so much effort and time into writing it.

I use an app called Buffer which helps schedule when content is shared on your social media channels, not everyone is able to wait around or work out the correct time when you should publish. Buffer solves this by doing it for you to gain the attention it deserves. This is another area where Google analytics can be useful, you can experiment with uploading posts each month on different days at different times and working out when best to post your content and how often.

Productivity Management

Picture this - your current home has a fantastic super-fast broadband connection, you have a pretty bad-ass desktop computer with a large L.E.D flat screen placed on a beautiful large desk accompanied by a comfortable swinging desk chair. This is all placed a small step away from a coffee machine with endless espresso at your fingertips. Working is bliss.

On the road you do not have access to this around the clock. The reality of the digital nomad lifestyle is you face the challenge of time zones, travelling between destinations and working remotely from hostel dorms, airport lounges and cafes. You will have to battle to find a WiFi connection, and a good one could be hard to come by.

You will have to create a system in order to adapt your lifestyle to adapt to a new way of working. Working from the road is glorious, your office can change every day, but it has its challenges and you have to prepare for them. Now that you have your first real sense of freedom running your own online business, one of the first joys you will notice is how you're in complete control of your work schedule.

If you want to work all the way through the night or simply do everything in the morning, it's up to you. The work needs to be done, but it's up to you how you choose to delegate it. Working 9-5 can be a thing of the past, or not if you prefer. Drinking cocktails in your hammock on a beach in the Philippines can become a reality. Just make sure that you don't get carried away by giving yourself too much freedom, work still needs to be done.

Pomodoro Technique

Structure is a good way of going about this. Working in small bursts allows you to get things done efficiently so that you can move on and enjoy your new freedom. This method of getting work done is called the Pomodoro technique. It's the art of working hard on a set task for 25 minutes and then taking a 5 minute break, before diving back into another 30 minute set. This can be repeated throughout the day, as you see fit, in order to complete your tasks. Working within a set timeframe helps you to focus, keep on-track and not to be too distracted.

You can look into this technique at the Pomodoro website: pomodorotechnique.com

Rather than packing an actual tomato timer, you can download an app that sits on your desktop and does the same thing.

This technique is one that I use on a daily basis and I find it really keeps me focused on one task at a time. The best way to use the Pomodoro Technique is to break up all of your tasks over a month into bursts of 30 minutes, some tasks might need multiple Pomodoro sessions to complete so scheduling these appropriately, along with smaller tasks, to get it all done.

Bullet Journal

I have created a bullet journal in my notebook and review this each month with regards to what tasks need to be completed. As I get new emails with new tasks I simply adapt the list. Each day I try to schedule a cluster of smaller tasks first, followed by one big burst, to spread the workload over a month.

You can get more information on creating a bullet journal for yourself by watching this great video: www.youtube.com/watch?v=GfRf43JTqY4

Planning a month ahead not only means you will always have your month planned out in advance, you also know what you have to do each day and what goals you want to achieve over the course of a month. You can set yourself ambitious goals and aim higher without pondering around with no plan and wondering what to do with yourself.

The day you become a digital nomad whilst running an online business and being location independent is the day that you are your own boss and you're the only person that can tell you what to do. This is a great personal freedom, but it's also the reason that it's important to plan goals, break up tasks, set yourself realistic, achievable steps to follow and work with them to complete your big projects.

Killing Procrastination

Procrastination is deadly force in the life of a digital nomad. You need to keep control and focus on the work ahead, or you will struggle to remain productive.

You will need to cut off distractions. Procrastination is one of the easiest ways to kill productivity. Sometimes personal will power is not enough to stop this, but that's ok, there are ways to help you from drifting onto Reddit or killing four hours looking at cat pictures.

Selfcontrolapp.com allows you to block individual websites that distract you from your tasks, this way you can block the unnecessary websites and still use sites for work, such as Wordpress. It's impossible to use websites once it's running, even if you reset your computer the application still works, it's very handy to use if, like me, you are easily distracted.

For further reading regarding time management, check out a great book called Getting Things Done by David Allen, the guru of productivity.

Productivity Zen

Make sure you dedicate yourself to becoming focused on the tasks ahead. Successful people keep focused and get work done, you won't catch them watching cat videos. Well, not until all the tasks for the day have been completed at least.

That's also important to highlight, you should work hard, but it's just as important to understand when you should take a break and unwind or you could suffer from overworking and stress.

It's good sometimes to stop and take a step back from work, drink lots of water, take some exercise, or anything to just clear your mind. Many use meditation or yoga for this exact reason and I really find it helps to destress.

If I feel I can't focus and am drifting away from the task at hand, I shut down my laptop, take a step back from my desk and take a walk around the local streets for a while to pick up a drink or a snack. When I return, I'm refreshed and ready to dive into the task ahead.

Sometimes when I've run out of imagination and I'm not feeling creative, I like to leave all my technology at home and head to a local coffee store with a pen and paper, order an espresso, sit back, enjoy the music playing in the background and the bustle out on the street and just jot down some ideas. Then, when I return to my laptop, I'm ready to go.

Sleep is also important. It's vital that you create a sleeping pattern that works for you and your workflow. If you can create an early rise system, then make sure you go to sleep early enough to get plenty of sleep. I feel I'm always most productive in the morning and that is the time of day that I normally set myself the biggest tasks. This means that when I have lower energy later in the day, I only have the easier tasks of the day left to complete.

You can't be in a creative working mode all the time, but you can develop methods and outlets to combat these moments.

Morning Rituals

Morning rituals are great. Over the years, I've found that I'm most productive at 05:30 in the morning, and I'm not alone in swearing by the early rise productivity session. Get up while the sun is rising, grab yourself a coffee, play some mellow music on Spotify and crack on with the tasks ahead. You won't face any distractions at this time as the world is still waking up, which allows you to get on with your work free of distraction. Normally I schedule a running session before lunch and so I aim to complete everything before then. This motivates me to wake up early and get to work, plus, it's a great feeling getting all your tasks completed before lunch.

What I like to do is eat the big frogs first. Big frogs are the horrible large tasks that are the biggest pain to get done. First thing in the morning is when you are most productive and motivated to tackle big tasks. Once you've completed them, you feel a great sense of achievement and you're able to easily complete the easy, more fun tasks after this.

A normal, productive day for me starts with writing. I find that this is when I'm at my most creative. For some crazy reason, all I need is a morning coffee and I can type out 5,000 words in one go. After a typing session, I then schedule an hour to catch up with emails, Twitter, read a few blog posts and then finally check out my Facebook (I try to avoid this as much as possible or I'll get sucked in). Then I go back to what I have written first thing in the morning, double check the content and then publish and share the article across my blog and social media platforms before getting ready for a the pre-lunch run. Normally my running time is spent listening to my favourite podcasts. After lunch, I have a shower and a siesta, then work on projects with clients in the afternoon/evening. If I manage to get a lot done, I might take try to take a break to explore a new city, meet up with friends, or just read a book. Waking up in the morning means I can get a lot of work done and enjoy more freedom later on in the day.

Work flow is important and you will need to look experiment with what works for you. Some people even wear headphones, even though they are not listening to music, just to avoid people disturbing them during a work session. Getting into a workflow is important or you might go off track. Set goals, get them done, and feel better for it.

Normally I only check my Facebook, Twitter and emails once a day for one hour. This means I'm not constantly checking them all the time throughout the day, but instead get them all done at once when my attention is focused on the task. I normally only allow myself to do this once the big frog is out of the way.

This is another reason why I turn off all notifications on all my devices during work time, so that I'm not distracted by all the notifications that come through.

Automation

Automation is the ultimate goal. You want to set up tasks within your business which can eventually be automated over time, this can either be done with software or by using a Virtual Assistant (VA). Over time you will notice that you are repeating the same tasks over and over, such as responding to frequent email questions. The best way to combat this is to create systems, such as autoresponders, which can be used to avoid repeating these processes manually.

Once your business starts to gain traction and turn a profit, your time will become more valuable and you might seek to outsource time-consuming tasks.

A VA can be hired for an affordable price via Craigslist or an agency and can allow you to focus more on the important tasks rather than time-wasting repetitive tasks that don't necessarily require your input.

onlinejobs.ph is a resource website that sources VAs for a large range of skill sets and prices in the Philippines.

smart office solutions is another example, which allows you to locate individuals in Europe that offer a VA service. This can be especially useful for tasks such as translation or foreign language skills; VA's have endless skills that you can utilise.

You can find VA's all around the world for a large range of skills that vary in price, you just need to work out what you would like to outsource within your business and the price you're prepared to pay to get it done.

The next step is learning how to best manage and work with your VA, which is just as important the hiring stage. You need to ensure that you make your outsourcing requirements clear, direct and understandable. Any work guidelines must be clear and straightforward to follow, otherwise your VA could struggle to complete your tasks to your satisfaction, and your time and money will go down the drain.

Chris Ducker (www.chrisducker.com), is the master of VA help and is located in the Philippines. His website is full of useful tips about how to find and manage a VA. His book and podcast are very useful if you want to invest some time into outsourcing your workload to a VA.

1,000 Hours of Work

Chris Guillebeau could not have put it any better when he put together the 279 Days to Success manual, which can be downloaded for free online.

He advice is that, from day one, you will have a lot of work to do, so spread it out over a number of months and work on each Lego brick bit by bit. It roughly works out to normally be around 1,000 hours of work to finally start making a living online. This is a ballpark figure that varies from person to person and business to business, but generally everyone chucks this around as the figure to aim towards.

Your whole business scope needs to be broken down into micro tasks that build the whole picture. Rather than stressing out over all of it at once, break it up and work on each piece at a time, and then set yourself a deadline goal. In his case it was 279 days, you can look at what tasks you have to do ahead and then lay it out and see what has to be done.

I highly recommend giving this document a read, many have found this resource useful, including myself, and thats why it deserves its own chapter (Thank you, Chris!).

Passive Income

Set up a business model/product/service, automate it, leave it and then watch it grow. Once you've created a passive income product, you can leave it to be automated, check on it for just an hour or so a week and watch the cash flow in. Once you've created one, start another and repeat the process. Some passive models will be successful, some will have a long tail financial growth, while others might flop. It's hit or miss, but by focusing your time on different models you can spread out your risk. From this, you can start to build a passive income empire.

Over time, you could even build more websites and branch out or try new things. You can even replicate the same business, but, perhaps, within a different niche or in a different country.

I'm constantly meeting new people who are trying new ways of making money. After a long lunch explaining how they do it, it's possible to start something similar yourself, that's why networking is the key to branching out. You've already gone through the process of setting up a website, so it will be a lot easier and quicker for you to set up a second website now that you've learned the ropes.

Take book writing, for example, my first book took me 7 months, my second took me 2 weeks. Once I knew the process, I could eliminate what did and didn't work through trial and error. You have a lot to learn while building a new process, but once you know how to do it, replicating it will be a piece of cake.

The most important thing is to gain value from the learning process itself. I may have spent 7 months writing a book, but not for a moment do I see that time as a waste. I was able to teach myself how to write and self-publish a book, a very valuable skill. As I gained this skill for free by using online resources and going through stories of failures, it took me longer but I learned the process.

I now have that skill for life and I will never have to pay someone else to do it for me, saving myself money in the long run. I could even sell a "how to self-publish your first ebook" workshop for cash. It's valuable to constantly learn new skills.

When I created my first online video, it took a month of learning to get it right, but because of that it now takes me 2 hours to create the same quality footage. I never have to rely on waiting for someone else to do the work for me. Instead, I can do it myself or teach someone else to do it for me if needed.

Constantly learning allows you to step out of your comfort zone. Once you learn a process you will start to pick up other skills more quickly.

Customer Service

Once you're up and running, it's time for the next step - answering emails and engaging with your audience and clients. What you're crafting is a process that you will now set up to help you in the future.

Customer support is also important. If you leave a message saying "I'll get back to you in 48 hours", they will understand. When you set a date and you can meet that target, it won't be a problem. Not answering a customer back within the time frame will upset them and you could lose a client.

Your customers are everything and repeat customers are even better. Loyal customers are more open to new product suggestions you have. Without them you are nothing, so make sure you keep on top of the relationships you have.

Have a contact page on your website and make it easy for people to get in touch. Don't make it difficult or require them to jump through hoops just to send an email - it's frustrating. Communication is key, as they might want to highlight a simple fault which you haven't spotted that will save other customers hassle. It's also a unique opportunity to speak directly to your audience and network.

Do your emails on the go. Managing hundreds of emails every day is tricky, so make sure emails don't take over your life by managing them from the road - it's easy. Apple, for example, has a great built in email client. You can download emails to your laptop, go offline, reply and then the next time you connect to WiFi you'll watch the replies fly out around the world. This trick will allow you to work remotely while offline, such as on long flights, and then focus on the more important issues you need to handle when online. Not being bogged down by emails when you have limited use of the internet can be really helpful.

Another trick is to limit the number of times you check your inbox. Make sure you are not constantly checking your email. Once in the morning, say at 9am, is a good starting point. If you're checking 4 times a day you can get bogged down with emails. It's important that you reply to every email, but doing so within 24-48 hours will not annoy anyone unless it's really urgent.

Standard office hours are Monday to Friday 9am-6pm. Take this into consideration when working with international clients in different time zones. Most people check emails first thing in the morning when they enter the office and rarely during weekends. Bare this in mind when sending emails in order to get a faster response from clients. By cutting your emailing time to just once a day, you will free up time to do other more important tasks.

Following a set structure will also aid productivity. It's better to do a block of emails in one go when you're in a good work flow than answering emails sporadically over the course of a whole day. The same goes for social media - try to limit your time to one hour, if someone needs to contact you or share something with you then you can check it once, upload it once and avoid the distraction of being online.

By doing this you're freeing up valuable time that would otherwise have been wasted. You can focus on a task and complete it a lot faster by following this strategy.

Customer support can be done on the road. You don't have to be pinned to one desk all of your life. Use the endless amount of free, open wifi around the world and make the most out of your new freedom. The downside of this is making sure your customers don't suffer, this is why replying when you can is hugely important. Don't leave clients in the dark, without them you don't have a business. Remember to leave auto responders on your email account if you happen to be unable to answer for a longer period of time, such as while moving to another location or taking some time off. This will keep your clients in the loop.

If the type of business you are looking at running is software based, which might require an instant response, create an FAQ (frequently asked questions) page on your website. Having your auto responder point towards this page is a great step to helping clients find a simple solution without your assistance. Then, if they need help urgently, they have immediate access to potential solutions. If you are noticing people asking the same questions frequently, then adding an FAQ page could save you a lot of time.

You should aim to reply to every email you get from readers. They are awaiting a reply, otherwise they would have not sent a message in the first place. They may even look up to you and an email reply would mean the world to them. Getting a personal reply will also you, it's a personal touch to add to this digital age. Keep it short but sweet, you cannot reply to every email you get from a reader with a monologue. One or two lines are adequate enough to get across what you want to say. It's easier to manage small input emails with a large impact with a couple of simple hacks.

After a while I tend to notice that I'm writing the same replies to emails over and over. Text expander is a wonderful application that allows you to preset text which appears once multiple keystrokes have been typed. This means in a matter of seconds, you can reply to an email with the exact information you want to type. Rather than retyping it every time, you can store this information so it is ready to add into replies a lot more effectively. It can be boring typing the same thing again and again, this little trick helps and your customers get the information they want quickly. Even your entire FAQ could be typed with just 4 keystrokes - magic!

Make sure you preset a nice footer for your email so you're not having to type out the same sign off repeatedly. Have it contain an ending message, such as "kind regards", followed by your name, links to your website and social media, and even a small logo. This helps promote your brand and makes emails look more professional. Many people you're emailing for the first time might want to check out your website and social media, you're saving them the leg work and pointing them in the correct direction.

It's a great idea to also set up an "About Me" page, which I also link to in my email footer.

Common emails I get: What's your favorite destination and why? How can I get started travelling? What books should I read? Hey, I want to get into travel blogging too, how can I do it myself?

These are common questions I get and I want to help these people as best I can. I was once in their shoes and seeking the same answers, so I'm very happy to help. Spend some time crafting a well put together reply that can be used multiple times, if they receive great content and advice they will appreciate it, and you're not forced to type out the same advice all the time, so its a win-win for everyone.

Setting Your Goals

Set goals for what you want to achieve. You should be ambitious and not scared to write everything down. You can do this by building a to-do list.

I use OmniFocus, which I can access on all of my digital devices and has great ways of organising multiple lists. You can also check out Wunderlist, which is a free alternative.

Do the big tasks first and work the smaller ones around them. As explained with Pomodoro and Bullet Journal you can first shape your projects into a To-Do list. Use it as a dumping ground for projects, ideas and items you want to come back to at a later date. You need to free up the space in your mind and write these points down before you forget them. When you are looking at this list of things to do, its going to look like a mountain, where do you start? It's extremely tough to know where you should get stuck in and what you should leave for later.

Different tasks will stop you from doing others, while some tasks, will be next to useless unless you have completed another. It's one big game of focus management and you need to organise and structure what you should do first, so it's definitely worthwhile to shape these ideas into a to-do list. Some areas are more important than others and some tasks may be mammoth compared to others which only take a few seconds.

Working on extremely big, never-ending tasks is horrible. In fact they can be really demotivating. Make sure that you break bigger tasks up into smaller components so that you can see and reward your progress as you challenge yourself to complete them. If you can turn one project into 10 steps to complete, then you'll be more reassured knowing how much you have completed and how much is left to do.

It's also important to fit small tasks in throughout the day so that you get a sense of reward when you complete them. This allows you to get your mind off other projects for a little while and focus on getting things done.

However, setting one day a week to get all the little tasks done can also be rewarding, while still putting in a lot of effort. If you can do a smaller task quickly and instantly than do it. If you're going to spend more time typing up the task on your to-do list than actually completing the task at hand then don't schedule it, just get it done while you're still motivated. There's no point in following a system strictly if it's just as easy to get on with the task at hand. This diving-in approach helps productivity and clears your agenda from accumulating lots of little tasks that could just as easily have been done in an instant.

You can use mind maps for setting up large projects. Map out the big picture in points and you will feel more organised, which will boost your productivity. If you haven't laid everything out for the road ahead, you won't have a path to follow, which leads to wandering and getting lost. Lay down a path you can follow and at least you can make sure your moving forward.

That's why, for every project, you should set up a mind map to chart out each stage of what you want to achieve. Open up each branch into micro tasks that help to complete the challenge at hand. As you can see from the Pomodoro technique, breaking up each task into micro tasks helps to organise the time that you use to complete these tasks. Laying out your tasks in such a way and then breaking them into time frames will help you achieve what you want more quickly than allowing you to do more.

For creating mind maps I use an app called MindNode. It's easy to use and great for organising your projects.

Writing up a business plans is a great step once you have dumped your ideas onto a spider graph and a to-do list. It will allow you to take a step back from the ideas you had in your mind and look where it might take you in the future. Map out what goals you want to achieve over the next 10 years. Don't worry about being too ambitious at this stage, it's good to be crazy. The higher you set the bar for yourself, the more you are likely to achieve.

A great book to give you a general idea of how to write a business plan is the "Financial Times Guide to Writing a Business Plan". You can map out where you want to go with your business and where you ideally want to end. This is smart, as you don't have to put all your eggs into one basket and you can spread your projects over many years. It will give you a vision and goals to aim for.

Having goals for one year, 3 years or 10 years from now helps you to focus on achieving goals both in the short and long term. Then, when people ask about what you're working on, you will have a clear vision of what you are setting out to achieve and at what point along your journey you are at.

Good Bookmarking

It's important to organize all the information you collect. You might stumble across helpful websites or useful articles that you want to come back to later. I use folders within my Safari browser containing bookmarks to organise all my saved websites into a more manageable system.

Pocket is a great app for storing web articles you want to refer back to later, which is helpful for finding articles you read and liked very easily.

1Password is another application that is great for storing passwords for all of your online accounts, credit cards and membership card numbers. Its a protective method for keeping all of your data safe.

I use folders within Evernote to read articles later on the road. I use Evernote as my digital dump box, I chuck everything in there to find again later, and it allows you to organise everything easily using keywords.

I also use Instapaper to send articles to my Kindle, for free, to read later.

Creating a system now to get on top of organisation will help you easily find useful resources again, later.

The Art of Adapting to the World

Running an online business is both possible and potentially profitable, but how does being nomadic tie in with this digital lifestyle? The main focus of becoming a digital nomad is to remain flexible and mobile, once you have an online business up and running it can be managed from anywhere around the globe.

Internet connection - rental agreement - round the world flight - finding a new social circle.

The aim is to create yourself a realistic path which is both enjoyable and manageable. You will surely want to visit different countries and enjoy new sights and cultures. You should also consider staying in a few spots for at least a month or two, to gain a whole different experience from conventional backpacking. This endeavour can be whatever you want it to be - you should embrace your new nomadic lifestyle.

At this stage you might not be sure what you want to do or where you want to go, but what you must understand is that running an online business can take you wherever you want to go.

Many digital nomads head to Southeast Asia, this is due to the low living costs along combined with good internet connections.

What you need to do is look, realistically, at what you're earning and where you want those earnings to take you. Australia is a great example of a terrible option - the rent is very high and the internet connection is poor for a first world country. It might be at the top of your to visit list, but laying low in somewhere like Chiang Mai, Thailand instead will allow you to pocket much more profit that can be put towards a future Australia backpacking trip.

It's best to aim for low-cost living destinations at first so that you can find your feet without financial pressure, learn how to juggle an online business while abroad and connect with a larger community of people already doing it.

Round the World Flights (RTW)

Once you have mapped out the destinations you want to visit and the length of time you wish to spend travelling, you might want to look into RTW tickets as a way to get you to and from your native country, via your travel destinations, all within one year. One great way of splitting this up is with 3 months in each location. For example, London - Singapore - Sydney - Fiji - LA - NYC - London

This route would set you back less than £999 - I've even seen it advertised as low as £700 during off peak times. As you can see, these destinations might not be ideal for low-cost living and running an online business, but they allow you loop around the world and visit many different continents.

The above route contains the most straightforward international connections, therefore its very affordable. If you start to customise your route, which is possible, it will likely make route more expensive.

So how can you make this cheaper default route work for you? Once you have reached Singapore, you're in Southeast Asia. Of course you could stay in Singapore and rent here for 3 months, but even though food and public transport are cheap, accommodation is expensive. What you can do is use budget airlines in Singapore to reach another Southeast Asian destination. You could even take a cheap sleeper bus or train if you want, then simply return to Singapore to catch your flight when your 3 month period is up. If you wanted to, you could even just book a cheap return ticket to Singapore then travel around Southeast Asia for 3 months at a time, for example:

Singapore - Hanoi - Saigon - Siem Reap - Chiang Mai - Bangkok - Cebu - Bali - Singapore

The world is yours and its up to you to make the most out of this new opportunity.

Finding a Place to Stay

Rental options vs. backpacker hostel

Renting is smart as you will pay one lump sum for the whole month. When broke up, this will normally be a lot cheaper than paying per day. Hostels often have monthly rates, but they won't necessarily be cheaper than just renting a small room or serviced apartment.

Finding a place to rent short term is not that easy as contracts can get complicated and working visas, or even residency permits, can start to come into the picture. You want avoid these red tape situations. Just keep it simple, play by the rules and you'll do just fine.

First of all, AirBnB is a great place to start in order to find short term rentals, you can find many options at affordable prices and you can even negotiate a better deal with the owner via email to get a lower weekly/monthly price.

You can also do it the traditional way, which works well in many spots around Southeast Asia - which is simply to book a cheap hostel for a few nights, then use those few days to walk around to different condo apartments and ask inside for rates and availability. If you're looking to rent for 3 months or more you have plenty of room to negotiate a better price.

Gumtree is also another website you can use to search by city for a place to stay - you might get lucky here.

Couchsurfing has many sub forums for people looking for a place to rent short term. I always have a look here as well, some cities even have sub-rental pages which makes it even easier.

Hostelworld, even though it's based on prices per night, also has many apartments for short-term rent on offer, so this is also worth checking out.

Just google a relevant term, such as "short term rental in Bangkok", and many options will pop up for you to have a look at. You can also add terms such as "digital nomad", or "expat areas" to each city to locate the popular locations for independent working. This is the simple process that I normally use to locate the best areas to live in for each city.

Visa Restrictions & Tax

Visa restrictions can be worked around if you can show that you will be working with your business online. Legislation is slowly being adapted to this new wave of online workers. When you are able to run and operate an online business, you can truly work and operate anywhere around the world and that's why online business is booming, it's a great time to join in.

This can be a bit of a grey area, as some nations are still getting to grips with what a Digital Nomad is. As all the work is done online with clients from outside the country you're in, technically you are not working in that country, you're working online. It's looked at in this way because working visas are usually issued in such a way that ensures jobs that locals could do are not taken by foreigners. Working online is clearly not causing this to happen.

For the most part, working visas are issued to foreigners that can take on skilled roles that not enough locals are qualified for, such as teaching English.

If you're working online with clients in another country, then you can continue to work on a tourist visa, but this is done at your own risk, its still kind of a "grey area". Over time these nations will work out how to deal with this new wave of Digital Nomads, but for now its good to remain open-minded and keep an ear to the ground for changes to the rules.

As an example, you can enter Malaysia for 90 days, without a visa, for free if you are a UK passport holder. This is just one of many global opportunities for location independent living.

You should always take the time to research current entry and visa requirements for different countries as they change all the time. Many digital nomads share this information online freely with each other so it is often easy to find the latest news.

The other issue this brings up is paying tax. Depending on which country you are from, working outside your home country may mean you have to pay taxes or not. Many digital nomads have started to set up business bank accounts in Singapore or Hong Kong because of their low taxes on digital products, but how much time you stay outside your home country can alter how much tax you will have to pay. I'm not an expert on tax situations in every country, but I wanted to include this as a simply a note as it's something important to consider. You should get professional advice from an accountant in your home country on how to best manage your taxes while working abroad.

Setting Up a Bank Account

If you're staying in one country for a few months it usually isn't worth bothering to open up a local bank account.

If you're staying for over a year though, it may well be worth opening a local bank account. The benefits are that you can be paid in local currency directly into your local bank account. I've found this useful when working with local clients.

If you can, stick with your current bank at home. Visa and MasterCard are accepted almost everywhere, and you should be able to withdraw your money worldwide - there is even a cash machine in Antartica. Just make sure you can access your bank accounts online so that you can organise your finances from the road. Most banks also need to be kept up-to-date with which country you're in, so come up with a system to inform them where you'll be and when you'll be there. This will help prevent them from blocking your card because they mistake legitimate withdrawals for fraud. It's happened to me too many times!

Some UK banks, such as the Halifax Clarity account, will allow free withdrawals abroad. As long as you can find a cash machine, you're better off with an option like this. I've opened two bank accounts abroad, both required some leg work and I didn't really get the full use out of them. Nowadays I tend to stick with my home account that has decent international benefits.

You can also look into the possibility of collecting air miles by applying for credit cards with air miles reward schemes. This might be a good solution to funding your flights while you travel around the world for free. This is especially useful if you're looking to get into a business where you will have to do a lot of spending - you can use these cards to earn free flights very quickly.

They work by supplying sign-up bonus miles that help you to collect miles every time you spend with the card. You can also unearth hidden secrets to unlocking loads of air miles by researching travel hacking. You can find out more about unlocking air mile secrets by reading blogs such as thepointsguy.com.

PayPal is the most common choice for transactions among digital nomads. It's the most easy service to use and simple to sign up to. It's also used globally, which means that a lot of international clients will be able to use PayPal to pay for your services.

PayPal is a handy tool as you can set up invoices pretty easily and it's straightforward to connect your

PayPal account to your current bank account, allowing you to access your earnings easily.

Other great features include a PayPal debit card that makes it easy to access to your cash in the real world, a purchasable PayPal card reader that allows you to accept card payments for your services, and a safety login dongle that you can use to make your PayPal account more secure.

Setting up a payment channel to your PayPal account through your website is also rather straightforward, which makes it great for quickly setting up a web shop using services such as Shopify.

Setting Up a Mobile Phone Abroad

Stick with the locals and pick up a SIM card. Don't get bogged down with a contract, instead opt for pay as you go plans with add on data packages. This makes life easier and you don't end up having to pay an arm and a leg to make local calls and use data.

I usually stick to data plans and avoid text or call credit as much as possible. With a 3G connection for on your phone you are pretty much connected to everything.

You can use Skype or Viber for phone calls internationally for cheap. Whatsapp, Facebook Chat, and iChat allow global free SMS messaging. All of these are constantly connected to the web via your 3G connection.

Skype is also great for many other uses, such as setting up a local number online that people can call and setting up a voicemail so that they can leave messages when you are offline.

Now this can be hit and miss. Some countries have extremely cheap 3G whilst others have sky-high rates. If you're happy sticking to free WiFi when you can and then buying a cheap SIM just with some cheap credit to make the odd phone call here and there then that can work as well. For me, if a cheap unlimited or 1GB 3G connection with a local number is not going to cost me more than €10 a month I think it's worth it. Many countries have 3G on pay as you go as an option and it's worth investing as a possibility.

It's handy to have 3G in order to stay connected while abroad. Using maps and local apps can help enhance your experience to discover more around you. The great thing about pay as you go is you can just get rid of your SIM when you leave without anything to worry about.

4G connections are starting to pop up globally, with many smart phones now allowing you to set up a remote WiFi hotspot using your data connection, which is smart when you need to connect your laptop and no other WiFi is available.

For US readers, check that your mobile phone is on the correct band in order to work abroad and also make sure you get it unlocked before you leave home. It's extremely tricky to get your US-locked phone unlocked abroad and can cost you a lot of phone calls and fees to sort it out. It's so much easier to have an unlocked phone when travelling abroad.

Creating a Global Social Circle

You land in a new city, you have your online business, you're going to be in Chiang Mai, Thailand for 3 months, you've found an apartment, the WiFi is working well. Just one problem, you don't know anyone!

Travelling solo is easy. I've done it a lot and swear by it - you're living by your own rules and can do whatever you want and meet whoever you want. It offers so much flexibility.

If you know how to, it's very easy to meet locals. Firstly, cast your mind back to any international people you've met while at home or abroad. Do you know anyone local to the place you're going to? After being a scout, going to university on two exchange trips, and taking countless trips abroad, I've been lucky to bump into many people from around the world. As you meet people you will start to build a global network of contacts.

This is why, whenever I go abroad, I think about who I know in each location and see if they want to hang out. It's so enjoyable when you meet up with an old friend in their home country, they always have the best recommendations of what to do.

Chances are if you happen to have a great friend in one place they will have a whole circle of friends for you to meet. I've found if you get on with one person you're likely to get on with their friend, too. This is great if you're living in one location for 3 months. You can branch out and meet mutual friends of friends, which will lead to growing your own social circle.

If you don't know anyone, don't worry, it's just as easy to make new friends on your travels. Everyone is more open to meeting new people on the road - it's almost a survival technique - so they're more open and friendly to the idea of making new friends.

Another area to make new friends is Couchsurfing, everyone on Couchsurfing has signed up for the sole purpose of meeting new people. You can even just use it to meet up with locals for coffee without sleeping on their couch. I've found Couchsurfing to a really enjoyable to meet new people and get to know a new place, because you immediately meet someone who has lived there for years and is happy to show you around. Perfect!

I did this during my first week in Finland and I quickly got to know a circle of 20 people who I then met up with regularly over the course of my year there. We would meet up in pubs, host dinners and go to the sauna together (a very Finnish pastime). It was a wonderful experience to be a part of something that wouldn't have happened without Couchsurfing. It's easiest to find these groups by joining the sub-group of your target city, which can be found easily on Couchsurfing. Many Couchsurfing communities have started to move away from the website and into Facebook groups, which is something else you should look out for.

This works in the same way when booking the first few nights in a hostel. Normally, when entering a country, you must state on your visa entry form where you will be staying. If you are going to be living in that country for 3 months (as long as the visa requirements allow it) then putting "I don't know" on your visa form might land you in an interview chair, which is not a nice situation. Booking the first night or week in a hostel will avoid this from happening. This will give you a place to stay for your first night so you can adjust to your new environment without worrying about a place to stay. Hostels also provide a social setting with a lot going on. Hostels get guests asking the same questions time and time again, so reception desks usually have loads of information. Just make sure you ask during quiet times of day when the staff are free and happy to answer your questions.

Everyone in hostels have a great story to tell or are up for a party or going for dinner with someone new. They're perfect places to mingle and get to know people. That's why I value hostels more than hotels on my travels - they just have a lot more going for them on a social level. Make sure you read reviews or ask friends who have been to the city for recommendations to give yourself the best chance of having a great stay.

You can also use tech startup hubs to connect with like minded individuals. You're going to be working on your laptop for long hours, so incorporating social events is important, or you can end up wondering why you are doing it? If you meet up with people doing similar things to you, you can arrange to work hard together at the same cafe, then play hard after. It's important that you don't get distracted by others and lose focus on the goals you have set. Mapping out the tasks you need to complete along with other digital nomads doing the same thing can help you to encourage each other, and hold each other accountable, with the reward of an ice cold beer after you've both completed your tasks at the end of the day. This is very similar to working out at the gym with a trainer or partner. Many digital nomads are interested in meeting up with one another. Usually, everyone that takes the steps to start a location independent lifestyle have some common ground, so you're most likely find people you get along with very well.

In addition, sharing your ideas and plans with others opens up room for discussion and inspiration. Everyone has an opinion and it can be refreshing to talk to others regarding the projects you're working on. They will also want to talk about their projects and you might have a different, creative approach or insight into their idea that could be really useful to them. Collaborating and talking with others is such a positive and important thing.

You can also arrange your meals around meetings. Planning meet ups for breakfast, lunch or dinner means you can socialise, work on projects, collaborate and manage your time better without distracting your own work flow. Connecting with a local tech hub or an online forum with location independent entrepreneurs and reaching out to other digital nomads in your city is a very smart thing to do. Don't try to complete the journey on your own - collaborate and you will learn so much and avoid going mad in a self-imposed solitary confinement.

You never know who you might meet - maybe a future business partner, or someone who can give you endless tips over a coffee to help your own business flourish based on their own experience. This is normally how these things come about, so network and get to know other like-minded individuals.

You can find new co-working tech hub spaces all over the world, with new places popping up in digital nomad hotspots all the time.

They frequently have fantastic WiFi speeds, good coffee within easy access, nice working desks, other nomads and arrange meet up events.

You can find some of these locations by checking out techhub.com and wiki.coworking.org. As more people choose to shift to a location independent lifestyle, I predict that more and more co-working spaces will be popping up around the globe.

If you would like to talk to other digital nomads, their are many online networks to communicate with them. Many digital nomads talk over a closed Slack network, which is a paid service, but is totally worth signing up for as their are many relevant sub-chats and even location specific sub chats. This is a great way to meet other digital nomads currently in the city you're visiting - check it out: Nomadlist Slack.

Reddit also has a sub-reddit for digital nomads: reddit.com/digitalnomad

And every time you set up shop in a new location, search Facebook for some location specific subgroups, here is an example of one Digital Nomad group in Chiang Mai. Just search around and you will be able to find a group in which you can ask general questions, find other like minded digital nomads and start to build a friendship circle in your new location.

I hope all of the above information is useful. I can understand that meeting new people at first is scary, but here's a word of advice - you've jumped out of your normal life to be part of this new lifestyle and flown halfway around the world to start something new, so don't be scared to go to a bar on your own and walk up to a group of people and introduce yourself. It's scary at first, but you'll get the hang of it, and it's almost always a positive experience. The worst that can happen is that you get blanked, or told to go away, but this is incredibly rare. Just keep your chin up and try again, you will be guaranteed to meet new people this way.

Head to popular expat bars in your new city, or look around your hostel or co-working spaces to meet new people. It's easy to meet new people on your travels once you get over the fear of approaching people. It takes trial and error, but over time you will get over this barrier and be building new friendship circles around the world with ease.

Chiang Mai, Thailand

Many global locations are becoming hotspots for location independent entrepreneurs. As more people adapt to this lifestyle and start to move to new locations, the places that choose to embrace this new movement will become more and more popular.

If a location sucks then you can just move. It's easy to pack your bags and move to another location that might work better. This is one of the great things about this movement - you adapt to where you are and whatever works. If something isn't working its easy to do something about it.

It's best to go to a location that is frequented by digital nomads when first starting out, so that you can easily find your feet. It's good to be surrounded by others doing the same thing to keep yourself motivated.

The quality of life, standard of living, local costs, internet speeds and weather are factors in the popularity of a place with digital nomads.

When it comes to all of the above, Chiang Mai, Thailand, wins hands down every time and here's why:

It's affordable - you can easily locate a decent one-bed condo apartment with a private bathroom and shared swimming pool or gym and security from around £120 per month, including bills. Their are plenty of these sorts of places around the city, just ask others for tips and wander around to check them out, they can usually be rented on the spot.

Then you have the food and drink prices, it's easy to find local dishes to enjoy for breakfast, lunch or dinner for less than £1 with water included. Not only is it cheap, it's cooked fresh and it tastes great! Local transport is affordable as well, you pay less than £1 for a long songtaew (the local truck taxis) ride to get across the city.

Costs of living with high quality of life is very good within Chiang Mai which makes it a perfect destination to run your own business, you won't be making a lot of money from the start so spending your savings on low living costs will allow you to go further when starting out.

With fast WiFi, a great 4G mobile connection and a large selection of co-working spaces and coffee shops to work from, Chiang Mai is the perfect destination for remote working.

Meeting new people is easy in Chiang Mai. Meet-ups happen on almost a daily basis. It's a hotspot for nomads and everyone wants to meet others to escape from their daily laptop grind. When you go to meet-ups here you will meet others doing what you do. It's refreshing when this happens as you no longer have to justify to others what you're doing - people get it and understand, it's great to surround yourself with like-minded people.

Thailand is also tourist friendly. You can get by with just a little Thai as most people speak some English. The only downside is having to sort out your visa, but it's slowly getting better. Before you depart for Thailand try to get a triple-entry Thai visa which allows you to stay for up to 9 months.

This is an example of one global location that works well for digital nomads. I chose to highlight the most popular as this will be the best place to head to in order to start out in this lifestyle. Meeting others already living this location independent lifestyle will help you massively.

To compare other global destinations for digital nomads, you should check out nomadlist.com.

Basic Gear For Digital Nomads

Travelling and working online is totally possible once you've crafted the perfect gear list. The dream is to fit your whole life into a hand luggage-sized bag using a minimalist approach. Travelling with hand luggage make travels easier and means you never have to lug around masses of gear from place to place. When working online you need to have some extra items to create your perfect mobile working office. Everyone will have slightly different needs - some may need large screens, others might need drawing pads for graphic design work - over time you will craft the ultimate gear list that works for you. You can find many suggested packing lists online and there seems to be gear that caters for each sector with mobile travel in mind. Below is the gear that works for me:

North Face Router - hands down the best bag I've ever owned. I've had it for years on the road now and it has never let me down. It has enough space to carry everything I need and has the right measurements for airline hand luggage requirements. I'm pretty sure this bag has another 4 years to go as well as there's no sign of wear.

Apple iMac 11-inch 128GB - I often stop and just look at this little laptop, because I have no idea how I've been able to do what I've done on it. It keeps on going and works like a dream. It has a stunning thin and lightweight design, which makes it perfect for digital nomads to use on the road. Its still powerful and you really notice the difference in speed and processing power that the solid state hard drive provides.

Apple iPhone 6+ - This fits into my pocket and does everything I could want to do on the go. I also use it as my primary camera for photos and video, and the quality is more than high enough for use in all my work. It's also handy for a number of other reasons, such as creating a WiFi hotspot. Having a smart phone allows you to cut down on a lot of gear and the endless amount of useful apps can make your life so much easier.

Amazon Kindle - Your path towards running an online business will require a lot of learning. Having an Amazon Kindle will put thousands of books at your fingertips and will allow you to read from the road. With amazing battery life, you can read for weeks without having to recharge, making it perfect for long journeys. It also takes up so little space compared with carrying even one book. This is an essential item I would simply not travel without.

Final Notes & The First Step

I'm not sure how long this lifestyle will last, but for the moment its working and growing. More people are looking at taking their business online and the community is inevitably becoming bigger. The only downside of this movement will that online markets can start to become saturated.

However, Eskimo communities have over 50 words for ice & snow. There are so many different ways to sell to different markets and with some effort you can discover your own niche.

There will always be new ways of making money online that come along. By taking steps now towards learning the basic steps you are placing yourself ahead of the masses. Self-learning is powerful, especially when it's put towards skills you can learn and earn from for a lifetime.

Being happy with this journey is the most important part of the process. As long as you are happy with what you're doing, then it's all worthwhile.

I've always stuck to the 10 year game plan that I mapped out back for myself back in 2010. I'm now in year 5 and I'm hitting all my targets. In 2020 I will stop or sell all of my online ventures and retire to a lovely log cabin in Sweden to roast and brew my own coffee in my little espresso bar to anyone who fancies visiting, just for fun, to meet new people and to keep myself busy.

It's okay to set yourself ambitious goals, just make sure you break up these goals into more manageable steps. Lay them out over time, focus on one project that leads to the next project and build yourself upwards, it's possible to reach your biggest goals by just taking baby steps.

The most important tip I can give is never give up. It took me 4 years of hard work to get my travel blog to generate enough money to fully support my travelling lifestyle full time.

Now, with all the skills I have now, I could achieve the same thing again within 4 months. It's all about learning, but it's important to never lose focus on what you set out to achieve. Never give up and keep on going!

Short cuts are tempting, it might be easier to chuck £50-200 to pay for a solution to your problem but the experience of learning the steps to solve that problem is far more valuable. You will always know how to deal with that issue yourself and never have to rely on anyone else. It will be slow from the start, but each day you can focus on learning something new (its all free online or affordable on Udemy) and start towards a road of building your own empire one step at a time. Thats the secret to killing it online and becoming self reliant.

The moment when you first make your first £1 online you will be jumping around the room with joy. When you pick up your first paid gig with a client, you will be shouting for all the world to hear. It may have taken you months to make that moment happen, but it will all make sense. Once you've got your first £1 online or landed your first gig, there's nothing to stop you doing it all over again?

It's not easy, it will demand a lot of work, sometimes around the clock, but as long as you're happy working for yourself then you are in for a wonderful ride ahead. I wish you all the best with your new venture, with travelling the world, and in creating the lifestyle you want to live.

Send me this tweet and join a global community of people killing it online - I'll send you a free goodie as well!

@traveldaveuk I'm ready to start my adventure towards killing it online and becoming a #digitalnomad

Best of luck with your adventure!

About the Author

My name is Dave Brett. I'm 25 years old and I was born and raised in Chingford, East London in the United Kingdom.

I have travelled to 85+ countries, studied in Finland, Wales and The Netherlands, and worked and lived in Singapore, Switzerland, Thailand and the USA. This has all been made possible by being frugal and sticking to a backpacker budget. I have no plans to stop any time soon.

I started a travel blog back in 2005 because of an agreement with my mum. Being 15 at the time, travelling solo was out of the question. I had the desire to do it, but my Mum was not happy with me travelling alone around Scandinavia. I agreed to keep my mum up-to-date daily with what I was getting up to if she would let me go.

So, it was either start travel blogging or don't go on the trip at all. Obviously, I chose travel blogging and TravelDave.co.uk was born!

From the start, Travel Dave was about my personal journey and travel tales. It wasn't until 2010 when taking a course in Entrepreneurship at Vaasa

University, Finland, that I decided to turn Travel Dave from a way to share my travels with friends and family into a business. I did this by turning Travel Dave into a travel resource for like-minded travellers seeking helpful advice for their own budget backpacking adventures.

Currently, I live a nomadic, location independent lifestyle which allows me to move anywhere around the world and freely go wherever I wish. I'm extremely mobile and never have a permanent location. I sold all my possessions some years ago and travel with a hand luggage-sized backpack that holds everything I own. I spend most of my time backpacking around multiple destinations over a set period of time using travel hacking techniques to save money and extend my travels. Between these big adventures I like to stop travelling for a little while and set up a temporary home for a few months in a new location. All I need to blog is wifi and coffee, which can be found all over the world (very handy). I plan on living this lifestyle until 2019 when I hope to settle down somewhere in Sweden - that's the dream!

Contact The Author

It's great hearing from readers, please feel free to send me an email: dave@traveldave.co.uk

I'm happy to help answer any questions you may have or if you would like to further discuss any points brought up in the book.

I love social media and you can reach out to me in many different ways:
Send me a Tweet: @TravelDaveUK,
Post via: Facebook.com/traveldaveuk
Follow my Instagram feed (@Traveldaveuk)
Pin on my Pinterest: @TravelDaveUK
Snapchat: DaveBrettUK
Periscope: TravelDaveUK

Backpacking on a Budget & Travel Advice

I hope you enjoyed reading my book Digital Nomad, If you would like to read more about How to travel the World on a Backpackers Budget, I wrote a whole book about this subject called "Travel Hacking".

This book will help you:

• Sell unwanted junk to help supplement your travel funds
• Pack like a pro and explain which gear you should take with you
• Find cheap flights in the most cost effective and time saving way
• Explore affordable travel options such as rail passes
• Buy food on a budget
• Manage your travel budget so you can go longer and further

It also shows you how to:

• Book Round the World flight tickets

- Use air mile schemes to purchase free flights.
- Use Couchsurfing for free accommodation
- Which methods are best for booking Hostels

Special sections concentrating on:

- Alternative sleeping options, such as sleeping in airports
- Looking into travel Insurance options
- How to study abroad
- How to Teach English abroad
- How to arrange Working Holiday Visas for Singapore, Australia, New Zealand, USA and Canada
- Should you travel alone or with a friend
- Keeping on top of health whilst travelling

Issues addressed in this book:

- Choosing travel as a lifestyle choice
- What it takes to be a backpacker - exploring the backpacker mentality
- Travel philosophy and beating conformity
- Using a minimalist approach to travel better

If this sounds awesome, you can buy Travel Hacking for Kindle, just click on this link:

Travel Hacking By Dave Brett

Have a spare minute? I would be extremely grateful for a review

Thank you for reading Digital Nomad, I hope you found all the information useful and I wish you the best of luck on your new adventure into a location independent lifestyle. It would be great if you could help spread the word about Digital Nomad by leaving a review to help other readers discover this book for themselves.

If you enjoyed this book be sure to spread the word, tell a friend who you feel could benefit from this book, or share the book on Facebook or Twitter and help others to discover it.

Thank you for your support in advance, it really means a lot!

Kind regards,
Dave Brett

Disclaimer

Book: Digital Nomad

Author: David Timothy Brett

dave@traveldave.co.uk

Cover Designer: Tom Van Altena - tominc.nl

(c) Copyright 2015 by David Timothy Brett

Notice of Rights

For information on getting permission for reprints and excerpts, or interested in a discounted bulk purchase of print copies, contact:

dave@traveldave.co.uk

Need a Proofreader?

I would like to personally thank Simon Partridge for spending his personal time whilst on his journey to becoming fully Nomadic to help Spell/grammar check and update this book Digital Nomad.

Without his help, this book would have struggled to become the book that it is today as he's made it far more reader friendly than it would have ever been.

In the future if you need help with grammar/Spell check work, be it for an academic paper, blog or to go through your Ebook too, feel free to email Simon and negotiate rates, he's simply done a wonderful job for me and I highly recommend him to you, thank you: simonpartridge86@gmail.com